Contents

Cindy McKinley Alder & Patti Trombly

10 Quick
Homework Tips

Cindy McKinley Alder
&
Patti Trombly

For information, contact
MSI Press
1760-F Airline Highway, #203
Hollister, CA 95023

Cover designed by Carl Leaver

Cover Photograph of Elizabeth Prell by Dawn Prell

Copyeditor: Geri Henderson

Library of Congress Number: 2020941034

ISBN: 978-1-950328-42-0

Photo by Ann in the UK - Shutterstock

Special Introduction for This Time of Unprecedented School-from-Home Learning

MAY 2020

Are you feeling overwhelmed with suddenly having to play the role of teacher (among so many others) during this unprecedented time of learning from home? If so, you are not alone! Being a parent is often tough. Working with your child when they bring regular homework home at the end of the school day can be challenging in normal circumstances. But now you might find yourself juggling your own job from home, taking care of the kids and house, AND playing teacher while the kids are doing all online learning… all at the same time!

In this book we will share with you 10 quick tips for making at least the school-from-home part of life a little easier for you. Though the tips are set up for helping kids with their regular, after-school homework, they all also apply to making school-from-home run smoothly, too. At the end of each tip, we will show you how to modify the idea for your school-from-home routine.

Hopefully schools will be back in session soon, but until then, try these ideas and see how much easier school-from-home can be.

Photo by ErsinTekkol - Shutterstock

Introduction

Have you ever felt frustrated with your child and his homework? In our 40 combined years of teaching, we don't think we've ever met a parent who hasn't felt frustrated, overwhelmed, or just plain confused about how to end homework battles at one time or another.

In our previous book, *365 Teacher Secrets for Parents: Fun Ways to Help Your Child Succeed in Elementary School,* we offered some homework tips scattered throughout the themed chapters. It is our hope, here, to gather the 10 most helpful strategies, all in one convenient place for you.

Overall, we have discovered that the main reasons for family stress about homework seem to come from two things:

#1. When and where to do the homework

and

#2. What to do when your child doesn't know how to do
   it

To help you conquer these problems, we have put together 10 tips that will help you set up some guidelines for
how your household can consistently tackle homework. As
with so many things in life, consistency is the key to making homework time less stressful.

Maybe you will find that your family has already implemented some of these ideas. Maybe some will be new
to your child and your family. Some kids will take to the
changes easily. But, if this is not the case, and you are wor-
ried that your child might resist, just remember that you
are the parent and you decide the rules in your house. And
if you and/or your kids are ever frustrated, you can explain
that you are making these changes so that it is ultimately
less stressful for them. And it will be. Just give it some time.

Ideally, it would be great to work with your children on
creating some of these new norms if you feel it is important that they feel a part of them. However, because you
are the parent, give yourself permission to make the final
decisions on what you think is best for your family.

With some kids, it might work best to ease into these
changes. With others, it works far better to just dive right
in and state that, starting tomorrow, these are the new
rules.

Of course, as always, you should choose what you
think will work best for your family.

Graphic by Cindy Alder

Tip #1
Head Off Stress by Being Proactive

*"The best time to plant a tree was 20 years ago.
The second best time is now."*

~ Chinese Proverb

Why is this Important?

One of the biggest reasons, if not THE biggest reason, that kids and parents alike feel stress about homework is that their family simply has no concrete plan for how, when, and where homework will get done. Kids may not act like it, but they need, and even like, having rules. They feel better, safer, if they know exactly what is expected of them.

Think about your daily life, at work or at home. Do you feel more confident, more calm, on days that you are unsure what your boss will want from you, when you don't know what you are expected to do, or where you should do it and with what tools... or on days when you know exactly what is expected of you, where you know just what to do, where, when and how?

Most of us feel best when there is a routine that we accept and understand. Though they would probably tell you different, most kids would rather have set rules at home, too. Rules about homework, specifically, may help relieve the anxiety that can come when kids try to postpone the work or get out of it altogether. If they know they cannot get out of it, if they know the rules and know they are expected to follow them, then there is nothing to try. There is nothing to bargain about. There is no confusion, no anxiety. It feels better for them. (And it feels better for you, too!)

You can start being proactive about homework by establishing some smaller habits, and then working up to some larger ones.

What You Can Do:

1. Create a special place for homework to go, such as a homework folder or notebook. Let your child decorate it to make it special and, most importantly, memorable. This folder should be brought to and from school every single day. At school, when he gets homework, he places it in the folder. When he gets home, he gets that folder out. All that he needs to do is in there.

2. Pack up the backpack the night before. Rushing around in the morning, yelling about homework starts everyone's day off on the wrong note. To avoid

that, make it a habit to have your child pack up his backpack the night before. Therefore, if something is missing, it can be located with time to spare, and in the morning, it will be all ready to go.

3. Create a Homework Agreement in which rules are set for when, where, and how homework will be completed. This will take pressure off you and your child. (See Tip #2 for more details.)

4. Also create a special place for homework to be completed. When your child has a place that is comfortable, distraction-free, and equipped with everything necessary to complete his work, he will be much more able to focus and complete it. (See Tip #3 for more details.)

5. Have a family plan for what to do if there is a problem with the homework. Don't have the right materials? Your night is just way too busy? You and your child don't understand what to do? Having thought about this beforehand and having a plan will help you get through it smoothly. (See Tips #4, 5, 6, 7, and 10 for more details.)

6. Think about your role in your child's homework. Some parents are involved every step of the way. Others like to stay out of the way. Though every child is different, it's probably best to try to find a balance: be available if he needs help, but don't hover or complete the work for him. Whatever method you prefer, just remember: always make sure that your kids are doing the work themselves; never do it for them. (See Tips #8 and 9 for more details.)

* Modification for School-from-Home Learning:

If you are finding yourself in charge of much more than just occasional homework, now actually trying to organize all of your child's on-line learning at home, these proactive tips are even more important. Having an agreed-upon plan and place will make everyone feel more confident... and happy.

TIP #1 TAKE-AWAY:

Spending a little time at the beginning of the year, (or even right now- there's no time like the present!), figuring out a plan for homework can go a long way to making the entire school year, or whatever time you have for school-at-home, run more smoothly and make schoolwork at home a lot more enjoyable for you and your child.

Homework Agreement

For Jordan McKinley

From this day forward, HOMEWORK shall be done...

Time: ½ hour after you get home from school. (Play time first!)

Place: First 15 minutes at the kitchen table to check for understanding. Then, at your desk.

Length: Until you finish. (Maximum time = 1 hour)

Solutions: If you get stuck:
- Look back at your notes & other work
- Come find Mom or Dad
- Check with a friend

Graphic by Cindy Alder

Tip #2
Type Up an Official Homework Agreement

Like anything worth doing in life, happiness takes time and patience and consistency.

~Mark Manson

Why is this Important?

That idea of heading off stress by being proactive about homework is perhaps best used in the creation of a Homework Agreement. Quite simply, this is an agreement your family makes that states when, where, and how homework is expected to be done. Having a plan before school starts in the fall allows you to avoid that "you against them" feeling that so often is attached to homework. If the year has already begun, though, there is still no time like the present to make a great change for the better!

What You Can Do:

Have you ever realized that it is easier to get out of something if you can "blame something else"? "Sorry we can't come to your son's piano recital; we have a family reunion that day." Sometimes these other things are real, sometimes, well... maybe not. But, usually, "blaming something else" makes it easier to do the things you really want to do and avoid the things you don't.

Since many parents are constantly frustrated with homework battles, we can extend that idea of "blaming something else" into the homework realm by being proactive: Sit down with your child and come up with a Homework Agreement.

A good Homework Agreement might contain these things:

- **Time:** When will homework be completed?
- **Place:** Where will homework be completed?
- **Length:** For how long should your child work on homework?
- **Solutions:** What should your child do if she gets stuck?

Because you are the parent, of course you could simply create this yourself, based on what you want. But it usually works better if your child is involved in its creation, too. To make one, try these steps:

1. First, find a relaxed time when all involved can sit down and talk calmly about homework. Take turns talking about what is already working well for your

family, and also what needs some improvement. Jot these things down.

2. Second, choose a time. Taking into consideration what you all want, try to find a compromise that works for everyone. Maybe you want homework done immediately after school, but your child wants to come home, unwind, play, and push it to the very end of the evening. Perhaps you can compromise. For example, maybe after school she gets one hour to have a snack and then do whatever she wants... and then it is Homework Time. A well-rested (and fed!) kid is much more likely to get to work than an exhausted, hungry one. Jot down this agreed-upon time.

3. Third, discuss where homework should be done. Your child might prefer her room, whereas you might prefer the kitchen table so you can be sure she stays focused. Again, is there a compromise in there? Maybe she can start out at the table so you can casually monitor to make sure she understands, and then she can go somewhere more comfy to finish up. Maybe there is a quiet space elsewhere, a place where she can feel autonomous but you are nearby. (See Tip #3 for more details.) Record this, too.

4. Discuss, as well, what she should do if she doesn't understand something on the assignment. (See Tip #4 for more on this.) Record your ideas.

5. Now, decide how long she will be expected to work on homework each day. Most teachers try to balance it out so kids are not overwhelmed, but we all know that isn't always the case. What does your family think is an appropriate amount of time per day? Perhaps ask for the teacher's input as well. Many have a one-

hour rule: if it is not done in an hour, they can stop. Maybe you agree, maybe not. Maybe it depends on the subject. But coming up with a general idea ahead of time, heads off a lot of frustration. Write down your agreed-upon length.

6. Use all of the ideas you came up with to type this Agreement up and hang it somewhere for all to see. (Try the fridge!) Now you have an official Homework Agreement. And now... you are off the hook. The next time your child tries to get out of doing homework, you simply point to the Agreement and say, "The Agreement says you do it now" and walk away. No more pleading. No more begging. The decision has been made. You get to "blame" the Agreement!

That is why this Homework Agreement is going to be a good thing for your child and your family. Once the Homework Agreement is implemented, there will be no more fights about where, when, and how she will do her homework! The pressure is off of you! You never have to be "the bad guy" again! From now on, you just say, "The Homework Agreement says to!"

But the really good thing is that the pressure is off of your child, too. If she knows there are rules, if she knows they must be followed, and she knows that begging and excuses won't matter, then why try? In no time, she will get used to the new rules and feel calmer knowing exactly what is expected of her.

A Homework Agreement is consistent. It creates good habits. And that takes a lot of stress off of kids. It helps the whole family see that homework doesn't have to be overwhelming.

- If you have more than one child, you may need a

unique Homework Agreement for each. Since every kid is different, what is best for one may be different than what works best for another.

- **Fun Option:** Consider using a buzzer (or an alarm on her phone) as a reminder of when homework time starts. Again, this can take the pressure off of you. YOU are not the one telling her to start her homework, the buzzer is. You get to "blame" the buzzer!

* Modification for School-from-Home Learning:

If your child is learning from home full time, then ALL of their work is literally homework. Having a policy in place is probably more important now than ever. You might consider adding a daily and/or weekly schedule to the Agreement. How much of each subject will be worked on each day? When? For how long? A schedule will help your child (and you) not feel so overwhelmed. She will have a place to look, to see exactly what to do when. Perhaps this will change week to week, but both of you will probably feel less stress when it is all worked out ahead of time.

Tip #2 Take-Away:

When so many homework battles stem from kids trying to postpone homework, or get out of it all together, (and parents are left feeling guilty or mean), there has to be a better way. Creating a proactive Homework Agreement takes the pressure off of the whole family.

Cindy McKinley Alder & Patti Trombly

Photo by Cindy Alder

Tip #3
Create a Special Place

If you have built castles in the air, your work need not be lost; that is where they should be. Now put foundations under them.

~Henry David Thoreau

Why is this Important?

Another important step to ending homework battles is to help your child get organized and create an atmosphere conducive to learning. There are several easy things you can do to set your child up for success.

What You Can Do:

1. Starting small, create that Homework Folder we mentioned earlier. Having one specific place to put homework to bring home, and then again to bring from home back to school, sets your child up for success. No more losing work, or turning in crumpled up papers. One important folder collects it all and keeps it safe.

2. Consider a Message Center for your family. If there is one specified place that everyone in the family can go to record important events or place notes to be signed etc. it saves a lot of aggravation over missing information. Maybe a bin in the office, a shelf in the kitchen, or right on the fridge. Where will your family look to collect important information?

3. Lastly, and maybe most importantly, to set your child up for success, help him create a good environment for doing his homework. Giving your child a special, well-equipped study space is a good foundation for quality accomplishments. When he has a designated spot in which to complete his homework, it will not only help him to be better organized, but offer him a welcome and ready place that is just right for producing his best work. It should be an area with enough space for him to spread out the things he will need to be working on. It should be a well-lit, relatively quiet area with no distractions (such as the TV, phone, or little siblings) so that he can concentrate.

*Something to consider:

How available do you want to be while your child is doing his homework? Being close by in case he needs help is a good idea, but try to find a balance between being available and being too involved. Of course, your child might have questions and need guidance from time to time, but be careful not to help too much and cross the line into doing the work for him.

Here are some things that would be helpful to have in the study area you create:

- Easy access to an online dictionary/thesaurus
- Pens, pencils (with erasers), colored pencils, crayons, markers
- A pencil sharpener
- A stapler, paper clips
- A notebook and loose paper
- A ruler
- A calculator
- A map of the world
- A comfy chair

* Modification for School-from-Home Learning:

When all schoolwork has to be done in the home, it is especially important for your child to have a special place to work. Having his things spread all over the house will not only be messy, but will also decrease the likelihood of quality work.

TIP #3 TAKE-AWAY:

Your child is much more likely to finish homework and produce quality work if he has a special place in which to do it, equipped with all the tools he needs. Work together to create a space that is just right.

Cindy McKinley Alder & Patti Trombly

Photo by wavebreakmedia - Shutterstock

Tip #4
Know Where To Get Help

Don't be afraid to ask questions. Don't be afraid to ask for help when you need it. I do that every day. Asking for help isn't a sign of weakness, it's a sign of strength. It shows you have the courage to admit when you don't know something, and to learn something new.

~ Barack Obama

Why is this Important?

It is very frustrating for kids when they come upon something they don't know how to do while trying to complete their homework. Getting stuck can really derail concentration for some kids. That's why it is good to know, ahead of time, what your child should do if she gets stuck.

What You Can Do:

Teachers sometimes use the "Ask 3 Before Me" rule. This means that before kids go to the teacher for help, they are encouraged to try to solve the problem themselves by asking/using three other sources first. At home, there may not be three other people to go to for help besides you, but you can brainstorm possibilities: friends, maybe even a pre-arranged "study buddy"; the textbook; her notes; online; a classroom site…

If it happens frequently, you might want to keep track of what is hard and ask her teacher for some specific ideas. Generally speaking, homework is used by teachers as a review of something they have already covered in class. Most often the information is not new. Therefore, usually, your child should have the prior knowledge from school learning to combine with her notes and book for help.

If those resources are not enough, and something is difficult, try to figure it out together. It is good for her to see how you try to solve problems, too. (See Tip #9 for more on this.)

You might find that sitting down with her to start a homework assignment, even just for a few minutes, gets her focused and off to a good start. It also lets you see if she knows just what to do or if she needs some guidance to begin. Just remember: it is always OK to help her out; just make sure she is the one doing the work.

If completing homework is consistently tough for your child, do consider getting a tutor. Her teacher may be able to recommend someone to work one-on-one with her once, or even a few times, a week. A tutor trained in teaching techniques may be able to offer more than just help with homework, but might also help your child learn life-long study habits, coping skills, and even offer fun ways to master skills.

* Modification for School-from-Home Learning:

When kids are not receiving as much instruction from their teachers as they normally do, it is more important than ever to have alternate ways for them to get help. If you are also working from home, you might find it hard to balance doing your own work and helping with hers. If she has a list of places to go for help, everyone will feel more supported.

Tip #4 Take-Away:

When kids get stuck on homework, and eventually they all do, it is important to have some tools ready to go in their toolbox, places they can go for help so they don't get frustrated and off track.

Cindy McKinley Alder & Patti Trombly

Photo by Gelpi - Shutterstock

Tip #5
Remember All Kids Are Different

Why fit in when you were born to stand out.

~Dr. Seuss

Why is this Important?

As parents, we so often find ourselves comparing our kids to other kids, to their siblings, to ourselves at their age, and - of course- to the outcomes on their report cards. It is so important to remember, though, that all kids are different. Here are a few things to keep in mind.

What You Can Do:

1. For this tip, we just want to remind you, give you permission to go easy on your child. If he isn't

reading as soon as his older sister, or doesn't have his multiplication facts memorized as quickly as his best friend, or even if he doesn't have all the top marks on his report card, that's OK. Again, balance is key.

2. It is important for you to be able to recognize if a bad grade is just that, a one-time thing. Was it a tough subject? Did he not study enough? Maybe he made simple mistakes. However, if you begin to see a pattern developing, then it may be time to dig a little deeper.

3. If your child seems to have consistent trouble in one area, or many, it is best to talk to his teacher. Is there extra help he can get at school? Would a tutor help? Does he just need a parent to help him focus on homework or study for tests?

4. Keep in mind that all kids learn differently and at different paces. It doesn't matter what his friend can do, or what his brother did at his age. What matters is whether he is learning, understanding, and growing as a student and a life-long learner.

5. Be generous with your time and with your patience. Praise your child for something finally accomplished, or well done, but always be sure to keep the praise honest and real. What will be most meaningful to him: praise for every single number he writes down, or praise for a tough problem finally completed correctly?

6. Consider meaningful rewards. Some kids will do their homework with no help and never need any reminders. For others, it is not so easy. If your child responds to rewards, see if you can find something that works. Don't we all like a reward for doing our

work? We might get anything from pride to praise to a paycheck. Kids might respond to rewards, too. While we don't suggest monetary prizes or toys, get creative and try to find a reward that makes sense. Once he memorizes his x3s, maybe he earns more playtime before homework. If he spells all of this week's words correctly, maybe you and he can bake his favorite treat together. If he finishes the book his teacher told him he has to read, maybe he could earn a trip to the bookstore to pick out one he *wants* to read.

* Modification for School-from-Home Learning:

If you are working with your child all day, every day, you are probably going to notice a lot more than you would normally if he were in school. Try to give yourself (and him) a break. Just do the best you can. Maybe after a long day of school-at-home you both need a reward for a job well done! Make a picnic together and eat it in the living room or outside and talk about all the small successes you both had that day. Focus on the good things. Let the bad stuff slide. Teachers are trained to teach kids; chances are you were not. Give him a break. Give yourself a break. Tell each other that you will both do the best you can each day. What else can you ask of each other?

Tip #5 Take-Away:

Kids learn at different paces. Comparing your child to others, or worrying too much about grades, can be very frustrating to you and create anxiety in you both that is simply not necessary. For most kids, whatever it is, it will come with time and practice. If it doesn't, ask his teacher for help. A little time, and a little patience, goes a long way.

Cindy McKinley Alder & Patti Trombly

Graphic by Maria Iglovikova - Shutterstock

Tip #6
Break It Up!

*Nothing is particularly hard if you
divide it up into small jobs.*

~Henry Ford

Why is this Important?

Some homework assignments are quick: Do these 10 math problems. Others, however, are much more involved. Young kids might have a project like creating a Family Tree. Older elementary kids might have to write a small essay. When your child gets a homework assignment that is not due the next day, but, rather, further down the road, there needs to be some special homework rules. Here are two things to make that easier.

What You Can Do:

1. Break up long assignments ahead of time and make a schedule. Offer her help before she even gets started by setting smaller, more manageable goals that work toward finishing the whole project. You might record those parts that need to be done in a planner or on a calendar. Perhaps your child would be motivated by having the steps put into a checklist. Many children (and adults) like checking off things they've accomplished and seeing how far they are getting toward their goal. This helps not only to make the assignment feel less overwhelming, but also ensures that everything will get done before the deadline.

2. Also, if one day's assignment is just too hard, you can decide to modify it or ditch it all together, depending on the circumstances. Ideally, homework should come first. But that is simply not always possible. Maybe your child isn't feeling well. Maybe there is no one that can help her. Maybe she has another commitment that cannot be avoided. As her parent, help her decide what she can and cannot complete. Perhaps write a note to her teacher to explain things and give a time when the work will be completed. Most teachers, if this is not a regular occurrence, will understand.

* Modification for School-from-Home Learning:

During school-from-home, many projects may be set up this way. Teachers might give assignments at the beginning of the week, and kids have until the end of the week to complete them. Without a specific plan to accomplish all of the assignments in mind, kids might be very overwhelmed. Breaking these up and choosing times or days to work on them is extremely important. Start by showing your child how to create a timeline or check list and move toward having her create them herself.

Tip #6 Take-Away:

Not much learning can be accomplished when kids are frustrated. Big assignments don't have to cause big headaches. Sit down together and break it up into smaller, more manageable pieces.

Cindy McKinley Alder & Patti Trombly

Photo by Lopolo - Shutterstock

Tip #7
Plan Ahead For Busy Times

Plan your work for today and every day,
then work your plan.

~Margaret Thatcher

Why is this Important?

Many kids these days have very busy schedules. With any luck, your child will still have time to finish his homework every evening. However, sometimes life gets in the way and there just happens to be a lot going on, on a big homework night. Now what do you do?

What You Can Do:

1. If this is going to be a regular occurrence, you might consider asking his teacher for help. For instance, maybe every Wednesday your child has a play-date after school. When he finally gets home and has dinner, he then has baseball practice. By the time he gets home and showered, it is just too late to finish homework. When you know this ahead of time, you could ask his teacher if it would be possible to get Wednesday's homework ahead of time. This might mean a little extra homework Tuesday evening, but it will also mean that nothing is late. It is a good life skill to teach your child: plan ahead!

2. If your child will miss school due to a vacation, ask for the work ahead of time. Scattering it out during the downtimes of traveling is a whole lot easier than trying to cram it all in once you return.

3. If your child misses school due to an extended illness, try the same thing. See if he can get the work and do his best to complete it from home.

* Modification for School-from-Home Learning:

One nice thing about school-from-home learning is that your child has the entire day to plan for schoolwork, instead of the few hours after school. Hopefully, this is one area where getting homework done happily is made easier.

Tip #7 Take-Away:

Planning ahead for the busy times teaches important life skills. As an adult, you don't get to choose not to do something at work just because you were too busy for a while. You have to budget and adjust. Showing your child how to do that now will be a skill that lasts a lifetime.

Photo by Flamingo Images - Shutterstock

Tip #8
Try a Role Reversal

To teach is to learn twice over.

~Joseph Joubert

Why is this Important?

Another great way to work with your kids is to try letting *them* teach *you* something. According to research, kids learn and retain over 90% of what they are able to teach someone else! In fact, William Glasser said, "We Learn...

10% of what we read

20% of what we hear

30% of what we see

50% of what we see and hear

70% of what we discuss

80% of what we experience

95% of what we teach others."

So, why not encourage them to take a turn being the teacher? One of the best ways to find out if your child understands what she has learned is to ask her to teach you what she is learning.

What You Can Do:

Show an interest in how her teacher is teaching math, for example, in the classroom. If you learned a completely different way, ask to be shown how it's done today. Kids love to feel they know something their parents don't. In some cases involving current practices, they DO know more than you! You might come to the same answer in a math problem, but there's a good chance you've approached the problem in different ways.

You could ask her to make up a quiz for you, and let her grade you after you take it. She will be demonstrating a deeper level of understanding when she makes up the thoughtful questions and shows you how to do something. She will feel good showing her knowledge in the subject, whatever it may be, and enjoy being the one who teaches you something for a change.

What better way to know that your child has mastered a skill than to have her be able to teach it to someone else? Letting her become the teacher also builds confidence and helps with communication and presentation skills, which are certainly beneficial skills to have in life.

* Modification for School-from-Home Learning:

When your child is learning all subjects from home, it would be overwhelming to ask her to "teach" you everything. Take time to notice where she is finding success in her work and help build her confidence by having her teach you what she's comfortable with. Then, when she becomes frustrated with a different assignment, she may be more open to you helping her and having you teach her something.

TIP #8 TAKE-AWAY:

Teaching someone else what they've learned is a highly effective way for children to retain information or master a skill. Letting them become the teachers also builds confidence and helps them with communication and presentation skills, which are beneficial, life-long skills.

Cindy McKinley Alder & Patti Trombly

Photo by Eugenio Marongiu - Shutterstock

Tip #9
Be a Role Model

Children are great imitators.
So give them something great to imitate.

~Anonymous

Why is this Important?

You've heard it before: actions speak louder than words. Consider, then, the mixed messages it sends if we ask our kids to do things that we ourselves are not willing to do. Maybe we tell them to make their beds, but we do not make ours; maybe we tell our kids to read, but they never see us reading; we might tell them how important it is to be organized, yet our spaces are chaotic.

The same principle applies to schoolwork. It is easy to *tell* your child that learning is important and has value, but *showing* him will go a whole lot farther. Let him see that no matter how old we are, we should never stop learning and growing. Let him also see you do "homework".

What You Can Do:

If you have work to do for your job, bills to pay, or a grocery list to make, sit with your kids while you do them. Let them see you doing work, too. (And hey, this is also a good way for you to be monitoring their homework without actually seeming like you are monitoring.)

If you don't have work to do, try just reading next to them for a bit. You get to relax, and they get to see you reading for fun! You can show them (versus simply always *telling* them) that reading is an important and fun part of your life no matter what your age.

* Modification for School-from-Home Learning:

Learning from home provides countless opportunities for you to model good habits and practices. Your child will see the importance of homework when he sees the adults around him also working from home. It's a wonderful opportunity to practice what you preach and helps build important habits for a lifetime of success.

Tip #9 Take-Away:

Don't miss out on all the opportunities during the day to show how you solve problems, work out compromises, complete projects, etc. Your child learns so much from watching you and imitating your good habits and practices. Never miss a chance to be a role model for your child!

Photo by Africa Studio - Shutterstock

Tip #10
Keep in Touch with the Teacher

Education is a shared commitment between dedicated teachers, motivated students and enthusiastic parents with high expectations.

~Bob Beauprez

Why is this Important?

Since you can't be with your child the entire school day, chances are you might be missing some important information about her studies. Therefore, it's always a good idea to keep in touch with your child's teacher, even when things are going well. Teachers appreciate parents who care and are involved in their kids' education.

What You Can Do:

If you see a behavior in your child that concerns you, or if she is struggling consistently in a subject, it's a good idea to contact the teacher as soon as possible. You can ask for advice over email or perhaps set up an in-person meeting. Sometimes, depending on the topic of concern, it is even advisable to have your child attend the meeting, too. Her teacher wants what is best for your child, too; so don't hesitate to reach out.

Talk with your child's teacher at the beginning of the school year and throughout the year as well. Don't wait until conference time if something is concerning you. If you are able to, volunteering in her classroom can be a wonderful opportunity to not only help out a busy teacher, but also see firsthand what her school life is like.

If homework is ever an issue, it's very beneficial to know the teacher's homework policy right away, such as when things are due, what to do if your child doesn't understand something, and what to do about missed work.

Working together with your child's teacher will help encourage her success throughout the school year.

* Modification for School-from-Home Learning:

You are your child's first teacher and if your child is doing school-from-home learning, your job is even more important. Plan time for scheduled breaks throughout the day. This will help refocus and re-energize your child. It will also give you an opportunity to reinforce the subject matter she is learning or answer questions she may have. Stay in touch with her teacher even during this school-from-home learning time. The teacher still cares and still wants your child to be successful. They can help with ideas and strategies to make her learning successful and even fun.

Tip #10 Take-Away:

Keep in touch with your child's teacher throughout the school year. Don't let too much time go by if you see that your child needs help. Teachers care, want to help, and have a myriad of time-tested strategies and ideas that will help your child find success.

Cindy McKinley Alder & Patti Trombly

Photo by Sunny studio - Shutterstock

Conclusion

Hopefully, after reading through these 10 tips, your family has several helpful ideas for how to make homework battles a thing of the past in your house. Whether school is in session and you are helping out with regular after-school homework, or if learning-from-home is in place, your family can create a plan and an atmosphere that makes homework battles disappear.

Some of these tips will be fairly easy to implement. Others, maybe not. But remember: give yourself permission as your child's parent, to set some new norms in your house. Even if your kids resist a bit at first, we think that you will soon see that, once the rules are set and the bargaining is taken out of their hands, your kids will actually feel better knowing exactly what is expected from them.

With a little time, some patience and planning, and a lot of consistency, your children will soon be doing their homework without all the battles.

Cindy McKinley Alder & Patti Trombly

Appendix

Checklist for Parents:

1. Head off Stress by Being Proactive
   - Make a special Homework Folder
   - Pack up the night before school from now on
2. Type up an Official Homework Agreement
   - Work together with your kids to decide when, where, and for how long homework is expected to be done. Post these new rules. The minute they are up, be consistent and stick to them.
3. Create a Special, Well-Equipped Place to do Homework
4. Have a Plan:
   - Where can your child get help?
   - What will he do in busy times?
   - What will she do with big assignments?
5. Think About Your Role:
   - Remember that all kids are different
   - Be a good role model
   - Let her teach you things, too
   - Keep in touch with his teacher

 Cindy McKinley Alder is a teacher, a writer, and a parent of two. She has a Bachelor's degree in Elementary Education and a Master's Degree in the Teaching of Reading. For the past 30 years, she has taught students from preschool through college. Following her love of reading and writing, she wrote two award-wining children's books: *One Smile* (2002) and *One Voice* (2013). With Patti Trombly, she co-wrote a resource book for parents called *365 Teacher Secrets for Parents: Fun Ways to Help Your Child Succeed in Elementary School* (2014). She has also published several non-fiction articles for children in various magazines. Cindy has dedicated her career to helping both her students and their parents make learning less stressful... and more fun! She and her husband live in Milford, Michigan, with their cat Watson.

 Patti Trombly holds a Bachelor's Degree in Elementary Education and a Master's Degree in the Teaching of Reading. Her many years teaching elementary school were in the upper elementary grades (3-5) where she was committed to providing active learning experiences and engaging students to bring learning to life. She brought her love of reading and writing to adults as a college instructor teaching English Composition, helping adults start the journey to reach their professional goals. She and Cindy's co-authored book, *365 Teacher Tips for Parents: Fun Ways to Help Your Child Succeed in Elementary School* is a collection of the most effective strategies and activities to help parents and children find success and have fun while learning. She is an educator, a parent, and a business owner who believes in the importance of helping children become life-long learners.

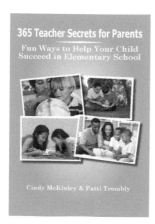

365 TEACHER SECRETS FOR PARENTS

FUN WAYS TO HELP YOUR CHILD SUCCEED IN ELEMENTARY SCHOOL

By Cindy McKinley Alder
& Patti Trombly

ISBN: 9781933455273

This reference book, written by two experienced and successful (and, frankly, brilliant and talented) elementary school teachers, provides a day-by-day set of practical ideas and activities that parents can do at home with their elementary school-age children to help them become better students while also having fun.

~~~~~~~~~~~~~

Recommended by **US Review of Books**

"An excellent book for parents to guide their children effectively." **Readers' Favorites.**

"solid advice for every day of the year" **Goodreads.**

From reviewers at Library Thing:

"the perfect combination of ideas and simplicity to become a useful tool"

"This book is fantastic!"

"This book should be in every educators library, whether in public school or home school, as well as any family library where the parents are truly concerned about their child's education."

"Cindy McKinley and Patti Trombly are experienced and successful elementary teachers and it shows in this book." **San Francisco Book Review**

"great not only for parents of kids in traditional school, but also for homeschooling parents" **Amazon**

MSI Press

Books in Our Pandemic Series

10 Quick Homework Tips (Alder & Trombly)

Choice and Structure for Children with Autism (McNeil)

Diary of an RVer during Quarantine (MacDonald)

Exercising in a Pandemic (Young)

God Speaks into Darkness (Easterling)

How to Stay Calm in Chaos (Gentile)

Learning Languages at Home (Leaver)

Old and On Hold (Cooper)

Porn and the Pandemic (Shea)

Seeking Balance in an Unbalanced Time (Greenebaum)

Staying Safe While Sheltering in Place (Schnuelle, Adams, & Henderson)

The Pandemic and Hope (Ortman)

Tips, Tools, and Anecdotes to Help with a Pandemic (Charnas)

CPSIA information can be obtained
at www.ICGtesting.com
Printed in the USA
LVHW050407221020
669428LV00016B/2056